Muscles

Injury, Illness, and Health

Revised and updated

Carol Ballard

www.heinemannlibrary.co.uk
Visit our website to find out more information about Heinemann Library books.

To order:

☎ Phone +44 (0) 1865 888066
📄 Fax +44 (0) 1865 314091
🖱 Visit www.heinemannlibrary.co.uk

Heinemann Library is an imprint of **Capstone Global Library Limited**, a company incorporated in England and Wales having its registered office at 7 Pilgrim Street, London, EC4V 6LB - Registered company number: 6695582

"Heinemann" is a registered trademark of Pearson Education Limited, under licence to Capstone Global Library Limited

Edited by Andrew Farrow, Adrian Vigliano, and Harriet Milles
Designed by Steven Mead and Geoff Ward
Original illustrations © Capstone Global Library Limited 2003
Illustrated by David Woodroffe
Picture research by Ruth Blair
Originated by Heinemann Library
Printed and bound in China by CTPS

ISBN 978 0 431157 50 4 (hardback)
13 12 11 10 09
10 9 8 7 6 5 4 3 2 1

ISBN 978 0 431157 64 1 (paperback)
13 12 11 10 09
10 9 8 7 6 5 4 3 2 1

British Library Cataloguing in Publication Data
Ballard, Carol
Muscles. - 2nd ed. - (Body focus)
1. Muscles - Juvenile literature 2. Muscles - Diseases - Juvenile literature
I. Title
612.7'4
A full catalogue record for this book is available from the British Library.

Acknowledgements
We would like to thank the following for permission to reproduce photographs: Corbis pp. **8**, **9** (Royalty Free), **10** (Ed Bock Photography), **31** (Robbie Jack), **43**; Getty Images pp. **26**, **33**; Photodisc pp. **22**, **24**; Science Photo Library pp. **14** (Manfred Kage), **32** (Quest), **39** (Damien Lovegrove), **7**, **11**, **23**, **25**, **41**.

Cover electron micrograph image of muscle fibres reproduced with permission of Science Photo Library (EYE OF SCIENCE).

We would like to thank David Wright for his invaluable help in the preparation of this book.

Every effort has been made to contact copyright holders of material reproduced in this book. Any omissions will be rectified in subsequent printings if notice is given to the publishers.

Contents

Words appearing in the text in bold, **like this**, are explained in the Glossary.

Introduction

Muscles are vital to your body. They carry out essential functions, and allow you to move all or part of your body. Muscles make up 40 to 50 percent of the body weight of an average adult man, and 30 to 40 percent of that of a woman.

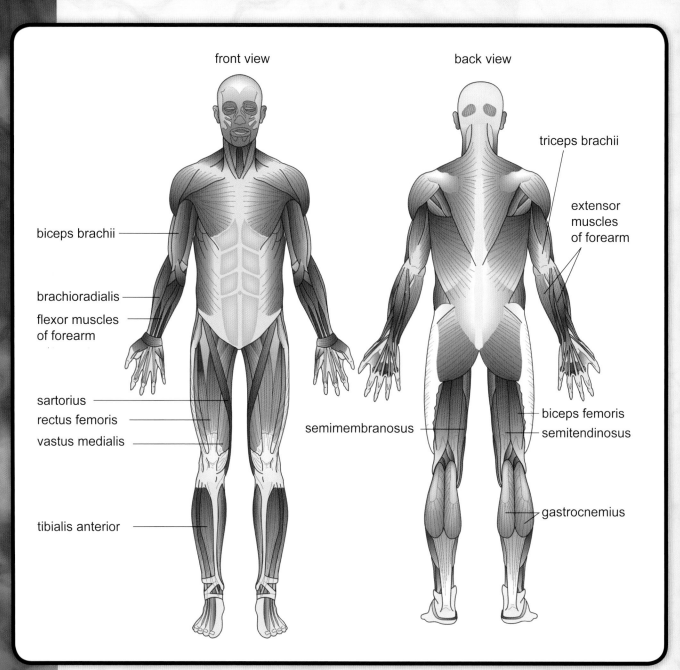

front view

back view

triceps brachii

extensor muscles of forearm

biceps brachii

brachioradialis

flexor muscles of forearm

sartorius

rectus femoris

vastus medialis

semimembranosus

biceps femoris

semitendinosus

gastrocnemius

tibialis anterior

 These pictures show the main muscles in your body that allow you to move and to maintain your posture.

The different functions of muscles

When you think about muscles, you probably think first about those that allow you to move. Most are attached to bones, and their contractions pull the bones into new positions. Some muscles, such as certain muscles in the face, are not attached to bones. Instead, they move skin, allowing you to move your lips and change your facial expression. Muscles in your throat move the vocal cords, allowing you to talk, sing, and shout.

Different muscles are responsible for different types of movement. The strong muscles of the thigh and buttock help you to move your whole body. Tiny muscles attached to your eye make very small, precise movements.

Muscles are also responsible for maintaining your body position. By controlling the positions of your bones and joints, muscles help you to keep a balanced posture. This is particularly important for sports such as gymnastics and ice skating.

Your heart is one of your most important muscles. It beats continuously, pumping blood to every part of your body. Muscles in your chest move your ribcage, allowing you to breathe in and out.

The digestive system has muscles throughout its length, which help to push food along. Other internal organs and vessels, such as blood vessels, also have muscles.

Muscles that you use to move all or part of your body are under your control; you can decide whether or not to kick a ball, raise your hand, or nod your head. Other muscles, such as the heart muscle and those in the digestive system, operate without your having to think about it at all.

When muscles work, they use energy and release heat. This helps to keep your body warm.

HEALTH FOCUS: Keeping muscles healthy

Food is important in helping to keep muscles strong and healthy. It makes sense to try to eat a balanced diet that contains all the **nutrients** your muscles need to grow and develop. Competing athletes will eat a diet high in **proteins**, **vitamins**, and **minerals** such as iron, to keep their muscles in top condition. Exercise is important, too; the more you use your muscles, the stronger they will be.

Different types of muscles

Muscles vary in size, shape, and internal structure, depending on their function and position within the body. Each is specially designed to carry out its own particular function.

Voluntary and involuntary muscles

Some actions, such as moving your hand, walking, and turning your head, are all under your control. You can choose whether or not to make these movements. Muscles involved in movements of this sort are called "**voluntary muscles**". Other movements happen without thinking about it. Your heart continues to beat, whether you are awake or asleep, and muscles in your digestive system push food along continuously. You cannot control the actions of these muscles and, as a result, they are called "**involuntary muscles**".

Skeletal muscle

As its name suggests, the main function of a skeletal muscle is to move bones. It is also called "**striated** muscle" because, if you look at it under a microscope, you can see it has a pattern of stripes (striations). Most skeletal muscles are voluntary muscles, but they can sometimes also act without your control. This happens when you suffer from a twitch.

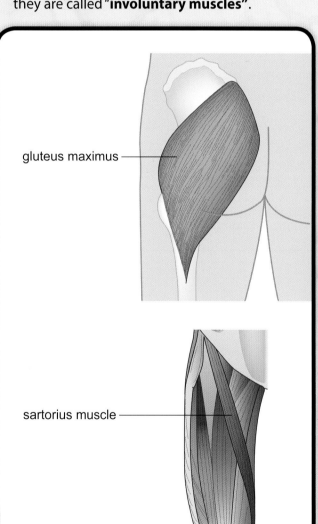

gluteus maximus

sartorius muscle

Skeletal muscles come in a wide variety of shapes and sizes. One of the longest muscles in the human body is the sartorius, at the front of the thigh. The strongest muscle is the gluteus maximus, responsible for moving hip and thigh. It is involved when powerful movements are needed, as in climbing stairs, running, and jumping.

Cardiac muscle

This type of muscle is found only in the heart. Under a microscope, you can see that it has a striped pattern, similar to that of skeletal muscle. **Cardiac muscle** is an involuntary muscle; its speed of contraction is set by its own built-in pacemaker, and it can also be influenced by some **hormones**.

Smooth muscle

The walls of some internal organs and vessels contain **smooth muscle**. These muscles also occur in the skin, attached to hair cells. This type of muscle does not have a striped pattern. They are involuntary muscles, and cause movement inside internal organs, such as the gut, and vessels.

This electron micrograph shows some of the cells that make up cardiac muscle in a healthy heart.

IN FOCUS: SAFETY SYSTEM

Muscles used in breathing are partly under your control. You can decide to hold your breath, and you can breathe more quickly or slowly on purpose. This could be dangerous, though, and so your body has a safety override system: if you are not taking in enough oxygen, your brain takes charge and makes you breathe normally again. Breathing too quickly means that you can take in too much oxygen, and feel light-headed and dizzy. Again, your brain will usually take control and slow the breathing back to a normal rate.

Healthy muscles

It makes sense to keep your muscles strong and healthy, to help you to get the most out of everything that you do. The food you eat and the exercise you do both have an effect on your muscles. It is easy to damage muscles, so you should try to follow safety instructions whenever possible.

Food

Muscle **fibres** are made up of protein molecules, which are put together from smaller molecules called **amino acids**. Your body cannot make amino acids – you have to get them from the food you eat. Good sources of protein include meat, fish, eggs, nuts, and **pulses**. You should try to eat some food of this type every day.

When muscles work, they use energy, which also has to come from your food. Starchy foods, such as bread, rice, pasta, and bananas, are all full of energy. Long-distance runners often eat a pasta-rich meal the night before a race, so that they have plenty of energy stored up for the next day. Fatty foods and sugary foods also give you energy, but it is better for your general health not to eat too much of these.

Regular exercise, such as swimming, can help to keep your muscles strong and healthy.

IN FOCUS: VITAMINS AND MINERALS

Vitamins and minerals are important for the health of every part of your body, including your muscles. Fresh fruit and vegetables provide all that you need. Bananas are especially good because they are rich in potassium, which is essential for muscle function. Calcium, found in milk, cheese, and a wide range of vegetables and fruit, is an essential mineral for muscle contraction.

Exercise

The more a muscle is used, the stronger it becomes. Muscles that are not used will gradually shrink and become weak. Like the skeletal muscles, the **cardiac muscle** of your heart also benefits from exercise. Dancing, swimming, cycling, running, gymnastics, and ball games are all types of exercise that will help to keep your muscles strong and healthy. If you can do these types of exercise three times a week, you'll soon feel the benefit. It makes sense to build up the amount of exercise you do gradually, rather than suddenly launching into a demanding exercise programme; this gives your body time to adjust and become used to the extra work you are making it do.

When you exercise, you sweat. As you sweat, your body loses water and you can become dehydrated. Try to make sure that you avoid this by drinking plenty of water.

 Remember to warm up gently before you begin strenuous exercise. This will help to avoid injury to your muscles.

HEALTH FOCUS: Avoiding injury

Before you start to exercise, your muscles are cold and stiff. They can be easily injured if you exercise vigorously without warming up first. You should begin gently, with a few slow stretching movements. Your muscles will then warm up, and you are much less likely to injure them when you begin your activity.

After exercise, a few minutes of gentle stretches will help your muscles to cool down slowly. This can help to prevent you feeling stiff and sore later.

Exercise and muscles

Exercising a muscle increases its size and strength. Different types of exercise affect different muscles in different ways. Exercise routines can be specifically designed to develop muscles in a particular part of the body, to improve stamina and to increase suppleness or overall strength.

IN FOCUS:
INTERVAL TRAINING

During interval training, a short burst of high-intensity activity increases the heart rate. This is followed by a short recovery period, during which the heart rate slowly decreases. Another burst of high-intensity activity is followed by another recovery period, and this pattern is repeated throughout the training session. In a gym, a typical pattern might be 40 seconds of rowing as hard as you can, followed by a 20 second recovery period of sitting still. Interval training mimics the pattern of many sports; in tennis and squash, for example, players will exert themselves fully while the ball is in play and then have a short recovery period between points.

When you exercise a muscle, it gets bigger and stronger. The muscle has no more muscle **fibres** than before you began exercising, but each individual muscle fibre becomes fatter. The blood supply to the muscle also increases, so that more oxygen and energy can be brought to the muscle, and more waste products can be carried away.

Aerobic exercise, such as dancing and jogging, helps to increase stamina. This allows you to continue exercising for longer periods. **Anaerobic** exercise, such as weightlifting, builds up muscle strength for short bursts of intense activity. Many people have an exercise routine of "interval training", which alternates aerobic and anaerobic exercise to build up both strength and stamina.

Muscles that are not used for a long time, for example, when a leg is in plaster, can shrink and become weak.

HEALTH FOCUS: Overexercising

Too much exercise without allowing sufficient recovery time can damage muscles. Scientists have examined muscle tissue from athletes before and after vigorous exercise, and have found microscopic tears and other damage. The levels of muscle **proteins** in the blood also increase after exercise, suggesting that they have been released from damaged muscle fibres.

Lack of exercise

Lack of exercise can cause muscles to shrink, or "atrophy". People who have an arm or leg in a plaster cast for a long time often find that, when the plaster is removed, the muscles are weak through lack of use. Muscle fibres are slowly replaced by fibrous connective tissue. This change cannot be reversed, but exercise can help to increase the size and strength of the remaining muscle fibres. **Physiotherapy** is often used to help people to regain muscle strength after an injury or prolonged bed rest.

 Astronauts need to exercise when they are in space to try to maintain their muscles' strength.

IN FOCUS: MUSCLES IN SPACE

Astronauts who spend long periods of time in space find that their muscles slowly decrease in size. Even though they exercise as much as possible, their muscles do not have to work as hard as they do on Earth, because they are not pulling against the force of gravity. The nerve endings of astronauts' muscles are also often damaged, which makes coordination and precise movements difficult.

Skeletal muscles

The human body contains more than 600 skeletal muscles, differing in shape, size, and function. Muscles can be named and classified according to their shape, size, action, and location.

Strap muscles

Strap muscles, also called parallel muscles, are the simplest of the skeletal muscles, and are not very strong. Bundles of muscle **fibres**, called **fascicles**, run parallel to each other along the length of the muscle. Some of the muscles in the abdominal wall are strap muscles.

Fusiform muscles

Fusiform muscles are fat in the middle and thin at each end. The fat middle section is made up of fascicles, which run parallel to each other along the length of the muscle. The thin end sections are strong **tendons**, which attach the muscle to the bone. The biceps muscle, attached to the shoulder blade and lower arm bones, is a fusiform muscle. When it contracts, the lower arm is raised.

Pennate muscles

Pennate muscles are made up of short fascicles. A tendon runs along the centre of the fascicles, which spread out in a fan shape from it. There are several different arrangements of fascicles and tendons. In some muscles, such as those that move the thumb, fascicles are arranged along one side of the tendon.

These diagrams show various muscle shapes, with examples:
- strap – helps movement of the head
- fusiform – raises lower arm
- unipennate – bends the thumb
- multipennate – raises the arm outwards
- circular – controls lip movements.

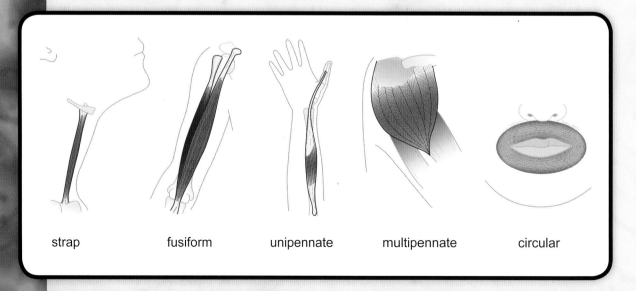

| strap | fusiform | unipennate | multipennate | circular |

In others, such as in the muscle that runs up the front of the thigh, fascicles are arranged along both sides of a central tendon. Muscles such as the powerful deltoid muscles of the shoulders have fascicles that are attached at a range of angles to several tendons. Some muscles are triangular, with fascicles that fan out from a single central tendon; this arrangement forms powerful muscles, such as the pectoral muscles of the chest. Some muscles are circular, with fascicles arranged in concentric circles. These rings of muscle are called sphincters. They control the size of an opening, such as in the iris of the eye.

IN FOCUS: MUSCLE NAMES

Although the names of muscles can seem very complicated, they tell you a lot about the muscle itself. Understanding muscle names is a bit like cracking a code – when you know what each bit is telling you, the whole thing becomes quite simple.

Naming muscles according to their action

An important characteristic of a muscle is the action it produces in the body. Muscles can be named according to these actions. Some examples are:
- flexor – pulls two bones closer
- tensor – makes a body part tense or rigid
- rotator – rotates a body part
- extensor – extends a body part

Naming muscles according to their size

Muscles vary greatly in size. They can be named to give some idea of how big or small they are. Some examples are:
- maximus – big
- minimus – small
- longus – long
- brevis – short

Naming muscles according to their position

Muscle names can give information about the position of a muscle in the body. For example:
- anterior – at the front
- posterior – at the back
- medial – in the middle

An example of a full muscle name is *extensor digitorum longus*.

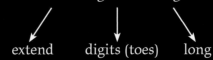

extend   digits (toes)   long

When you break down the name like this, you can work out that it is a long muscle that extends the toes.

Inside a muscle

Muscles are made up of separate strands, or **fibres**, bundled together and surrounded by layers of membranes. Blood vessels carry oxygen and other **nutrients** to the muscle, and remove waste products. Nerves carry signals from the brain to stimulate the muscles to contract.

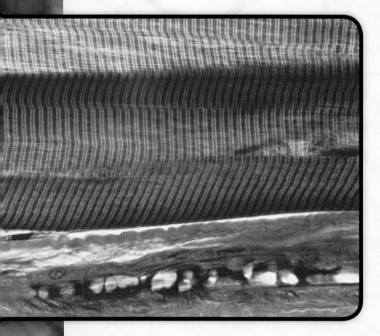

↑ This photomicrograph shows the striated pattern of skeletal muscle, made by the overlapping of the myofilaments.

Skeletal muscle

A skeletal muscle is surrounded and protected by an outer layer, called the **epimysium**. Within this, individual muscle fibres are bound together into bundles called fascicles. In turn, each fascicle is surrounded by a protective layer, and the spaces between fascicles are filled with connective tissue. This contains blood **capillaries**, which supply the individual fibres with nutrients and oxygen, and remove waste products made by the muscle as it contracts.

A fascicle can contain anything from 10 to 100 muscle fibres. Each fibre within a fascicle is surrounded by its own outer layer, the **sarcolemma**. A muscle fibre is one elongated single cell, containing tiny threads called **myofibrils**. These extend the full length of the muscle fibre.

In turn, each myofibril is made up of even smaller structures called **myofilaments**. These do not extend the full length of the muscle fibre, but are arranged one after another in a line, rather like separate carriages that link together to make a complete train. The compartments, called sarcomeres, are separated from each other at either end by narrow plates called Z discs (see the diagram on page 20).

Different myofilaments

There are two types of myofilament: thick myofilaments and thin myofilaments. Each are made from different **proteins**. The thick myofilaments are largely made up of **myosin** and the thin myofilaments are largely made up of **actin**. There are twice as many thin myofilaments as thick myofilaments, arranged with the thin filaments attached to the Z disc and the thick filaments sandwiched between them. When the muscle contracts, the thick and thin myofilaments overlap each other and, when the muscle relaxes, they slide apart.

It is the overlapping of the thick and thin myofilaments that gives the muscle its **striated** appearance. Light patches appear where there are thin myofilaments alone, and dark patches appear where the thick and thin myofilaments overlap.

Motor neurones

Motor neurones, carrying signals from the brain to the muscle, are linked to each muscle fibre. The neurone connects with a point on the muscle fibre wall called a **motor end plate**, which contains receptors for **acetylcholine** (a chemical released by neurones).

Cardiac muscle

The smallest elements of **cardiac muscle** are thick and thin myofilaments, just as in skeletal muscle. The myofilaments overlap, creating a striated pattern similar to that of skeletal muscle. However, the fibres of cardiac muscle are cylindrical and are joined to neighbouring fibres to form a branching network.

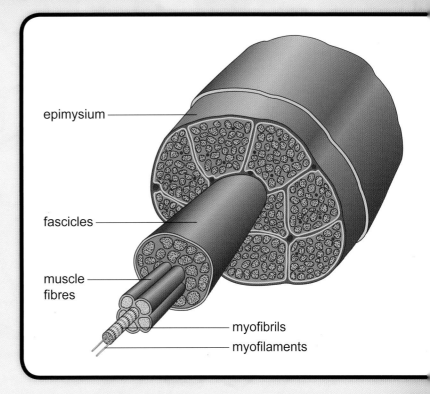

epimysium

fascicles

muscle fibres

myofibrils

myofilaments

 This diagram shows how a skeletal muscle is made up:

- the epimysium surrounds the entire muscle
- muscle fibres are bound together to form fascicles
- myofibrils are bound together to form muscle fibres
- myofibrils are made from overlapping myofilaments.

IN FOCUS: SMOOTH MUSCLE

Smooth muscle is also made up of thick and thin myofilaments. They are not arranged as regularly as those in skeletal and cardiac muscle, so there are no striations. Muscle fibres in smooth muscle are much smaller than those of skeletal muscle. In some smooth muscles, the fibres are linked to each other while, in other smooth muscles, the fibres are completely independent of each other.

Muscle attachments

Muscles allow us to move by pulling our bones. To do this, they have to be attached to bones.

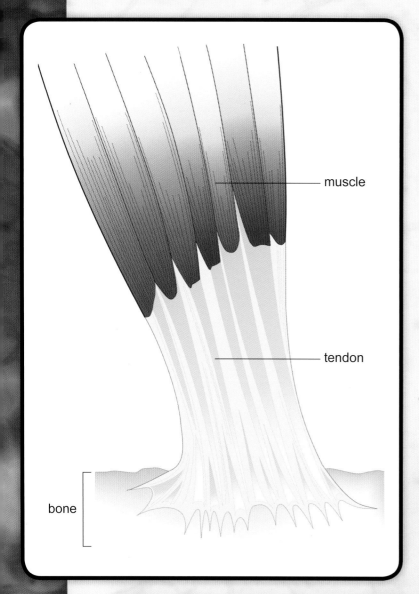

muscle

tendon

bone

Most muscles are attached to a bone by a **tendon**. This is a strong cord, made from the fusing together of membranes that surround the **fascicles** of the muscle. Tendons extend into the outer covering layer of the bone, and some even extend into the outer layer of the bone itself. Tendons make the muscle longer by extending from each end of the muscle. They also reduce strain on the muscle itself.

The thickest tendon in the human body is the calcaneal tendon, usually known as the Achilles tendon. It attaches the calf muscle to the heel bone.

 This diagram shows how a muscle may be attached to a bone.

IN FOCUS: OTHER ATTACHMENTS

Not all muscles are attached by cord-like tendons. In the abdominal wall, the tendon is spread out into a flat sheet, which is attached to the muscles or tissue lying beneath it. Many muscles in the face are attached directly to skin, which allows us to change our facial expression by pulling the skin into new positions.

Tendon problems

There are several common problems associated with tendons, including:

● **Tendinitis**: most common in the shoulder, heel, or hamstring (at the back of the thigh). This is a painful inflammation of a tendon or its surrounding membrane. It is often the result of a sports injury or a strain on the tendon. "Tennis elbow" affects people who rotate their forearms a lot, particularly in racquet sports. The tendon **fibres** become inflamed at the attachment to the elbow joint.

● **Impingement Syndrome**: this causes shoulder pain in people who use a repetitive, overhead action, as in swimming, basketball, and volleyball. The action repeatedly crushes a tendon between the upper arm bone and the shoulder blade, causing inflammation and pain. It can eventually result in a rotator cuff injury, where the tendon degenerates and tears away from the bone, and an operation becomes necessary to repair the damage.

● **Deep cut**: tendons, especially in the hand or foot, wrist, or ankle (where they lie just below the surface) can be severed by a deep cut. Usually, the two ends can be successfully sewn back together, although full strength may not always be restored.

● **Extreme tension**: overstretching or jerking can damage a tendon, because some of the fibres anchoring it to the bone get pulled away. It can be treated with ice packs and rest, and support given with bandages if needed. Sometimes, a plaster cast is used to minimize movement and allow the tendon to heal naturally. An operation to reinforce the damaged area with **carbon fibres** can give the tendon extra strength.

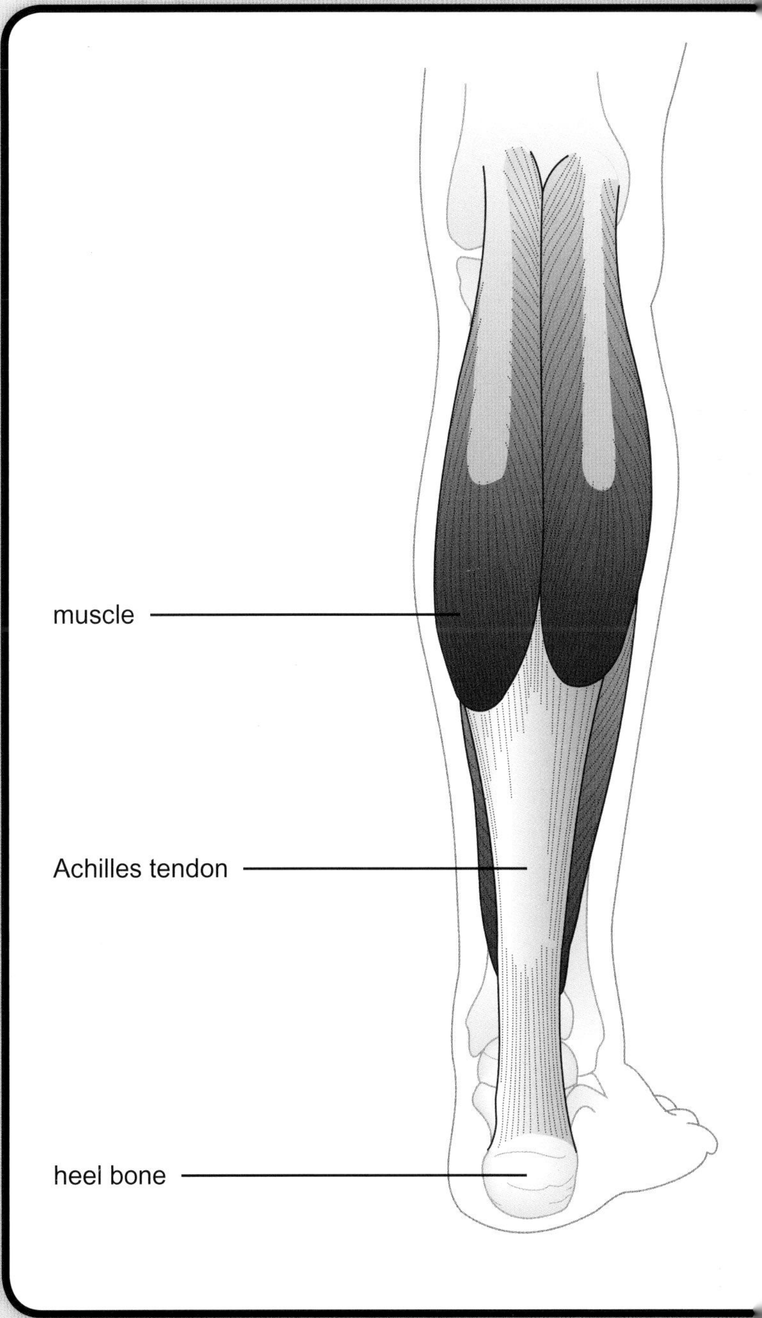

muscle

Achilles tendon

heel bone

This diagram shows how the Achilles tendon links the calf muscle to the heel bone.

Working muscles

Most skeletal muscles work in pairs, each doing the job opposite to the other. When one muscle in a pair contracts, it stretches the other muscle, and vice versa.

Arm movement

The up and down movements of your lower arm are controlled by a pair of muscles. The biceps muscle is at the front of your upper arm and the triceps muscle is at the back. Both muscles are attached to the shoulder blade, the upper arm bone (humerus) and the lower arm bones.

When the biceps contracts, it pulls the lower arm bones up and stretches the triceps. When the triceps contracts, the opposite happens – the lower arm bones are pulled down and the biceps is stretched.

The same type of mechanism operates in many other situations, for example, when you nod your head up and down, or raise and lower your leg. Two muscles that work together in this way are called an "antagonistic pair".

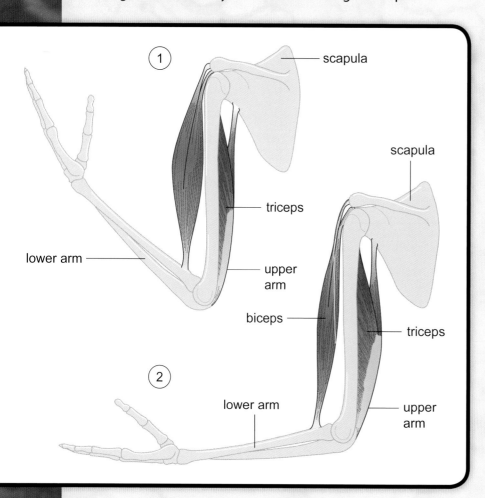

These diagrams show how the biceps and triceps muscles work together to raise and lower the arm:
1 biceps contracts, arm pulled up, triceps stretched
2 triceps contracts, arm pulled down, biceps stretched

A system of levers

Muscle movements work in the same way as a system of levers. A lever arm (the bone) pivots around a fulcrum (the joint). Two forces act on the lever arm: the weight that has to be moved (the body or body part) and the pull of the muscle. There are three ways in which a lever system can work:

1. **First class levers**: operate like a seesaw. The weight is at one end of the lever arm, the fulcrum is in the middle and the force is at the other end. There are not many systems like this in the human body, but one is the head on the spine. When you lift your head, the weight that is to be moved is the back of your skull, the fulcrum is the joint between your skull and spine and the lifting force is provided by your neck muscles.

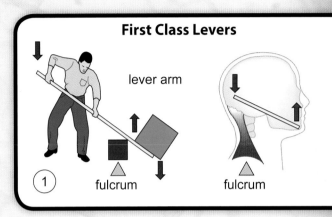

2. **Second class levers**: operate like a man pushing a wheelbarrow. The force is at one end of the lever arm, the fulcrum is at the other end and the weight is in between. These systems do not allow fast, large movements, but they can provide a strong force. Again, these are not common in the human body, but one example is when you raise yourself to stand on tiptoe. The contraction of the calf muscles provides the lifting force, the ball of the foot acts as the fulcrum and the body's weight pushes down in between.

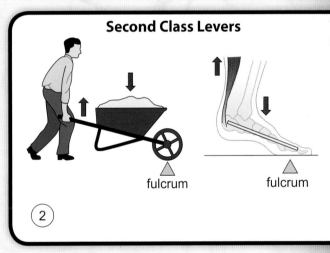

3. **Third class levers**: operate like a man lifting a weight on the end of a spade. The weight is at one end of the lever arm, the fulcrum is at the other end and the force is in between. This is the most common system in the human body, providing speed and a wide range of movement, but little strength. Picking an object up in your hand uses this system. The object is the weight, the fulcrum is the elbow joint, and the lifting force is provided by the contraction of the biceps muscle.

The three different lever systems are shown in these diagrams.

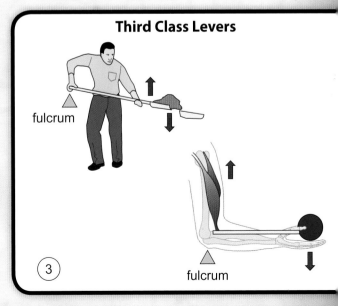

When a muscle contracts

Skeletal muscles contract in response to a signal from the brain. The tiny **myofilaments** that make up the muscle **fibres** slide past each other, making the muscle shorter.

The contraction of a muscle is controlled by signals from the brain, which are carried to the muscle by nerves called **motor neurones**. Each neurone is linked to several muscle fibres. One motor neurone and all the muscle fibres it is linked to are called a "**motor unit**". The fibres in a motor unit are usually spread evenly throughout a muscle. All the fibres in a motor unit receive the same signal, which makes them contract at the same time. The smallest signal that will make a motor unit contract is called its threshold stimulus.

"All or nothing" principle

The mechanism operates on an "all or nothing" principle: if the signal is below the threshold, the motor unit will not respond and there will be no contraction. If the signal is greater than the threshold, the whole motor unit will contract. It does not make any difference if the signal is just a tiny amount bigger than the threshold or many times greater than the threshold, the response is exactly the same.

Small or large force?

Different motor units have different thresholds, with some responding to a much smaller stimulus than others. If the work to be done only needs a small force, a small signal from the brain stimulates just those motor units with a low threshold. If a more powerful force is required, the brain will send a stronger signal that will stimulate more motor units. For the most powerful force, a very strong signal will be sent, and all the motor units that make up the muscle will be stimulated to contract.

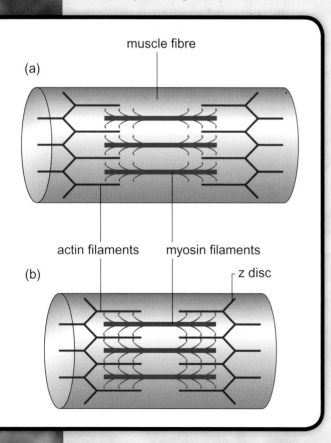

muscle fibre

(a)

actin filaments   myosin filaments

(b)

z disc

In the top diagram (a), the muscle fibre is relaxed. In the bottom diagram (b), the myosin filaments have pulled the actin filaments over them, making the muscle fibre shorter.

Motor end plates

The junction between a motor neurone and muscle fibre is called a **motor end plate**. When the neurone carries a signal to the motor end plate, a chemical is released, which stimulates the fibres to contract.

A. A signal from the brain is carried by the motor neurone to the muscle fibres. The thick **myosin myofilaments** in the muscle "walk" along the thin **actin** myofilaments, pulling them towards each other and making the muscle shorter.

B. Chemical bridges form, holding the filaments in place.

C. The muscle fibres only contract for a short time, and will relax unless they receive another signal from the brain telling them to maintain the contraction.

D. When the muscle relaxes, the chemical bridges break down, and the myosin filaments slide back past the actin filaments in the opposite direction, making the muscle longer.

How does a muscle contract and relax?

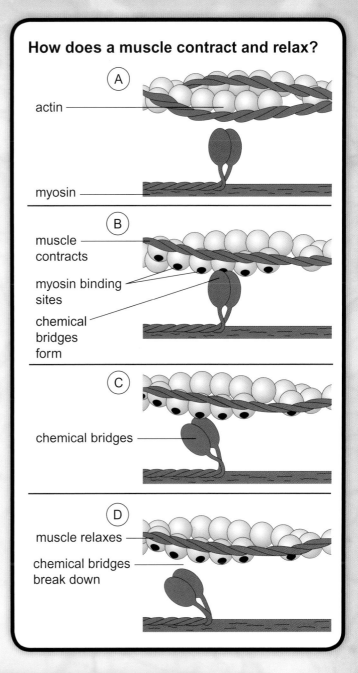

A
actin
myosin

B
muscle contracts
myosin binding sites
chemical bridges form

C
chemical bridges

D
muscle relaxes
chemical bridges break down

IN FOCUS: USING ENERGY

Muscle fibres need a chemical called adenosine triphosphate (ATP) in order to contract. As they contract, they break down the ATP into another chemical called ADP (adenosine diphosphate). The process releases the energy that the muscles need for contracting. Both these chemicals are produced in the body's cells.

After an ATP molecule has been broken down to ADP and released its energy, it needs to be quickly changed back (re-energised) to ATP so that it can be used again. The energy to do this usually comes from aerobic respiration. This process uses oxygen in the complete breakdown of glucose to carbon dioxide and water, to release energy.

Athletes' muscles

Athletes train to make sure that their muscles are in prime condition, to enable them to attain the highest possible standards of performance. There are differences between the muscles of different people, making them better suited to different activities. Some drugs can increase muscle performance, but it is illegal for people competing in sporting events to take them.

Different types of muscle **fibres** contract at different rates. Fast-twitch fibres contract very quickly, while slow-twitch fibres contract more slowly. Different people may have different ratios of fast-twitch and slow-twitch fibres.

Slow-twitch fibres (Type I fibres)

These fibres produce long, steady contractions, and can maintain their effort for long periods of time without becoming **fatigued**. They have more blood capillaries than fast-twitch fibres, giving them a red appearance – hence their name, "red muscle". They also contain large amounts of myoglobin, which ensures that there is a good supply of oxygen. The slow-twitch fibres use oxygen when they use stored energy, and blood capillaries carry away waste products efficiently.

Fast-twitch fibres (Type II fibres)

These fibres are good at producing short bursts of intense speed or force. They are often called "white muscle" because they contain relatively few blood capillaries and, therefore, they look pale. They also contain only small amounts of myoglobin, a protein that can provide a small store of oxygen within the muscle. The fast-twitch fibres use stored energy without using oxygen. Waste products build up quickly, and the fibres soon become fatigued.

Long-distance runners need muscles that can work for long periods of time. Sprinters need muscles that provide short bursts of intense activity.

Different fibres for different activities

The fast-twitch and slow-twitch fibres are best suited to different types of activity. Fast-twitch fibres allow short, intense bursts of activity, such as sprinting very fast for a short distance, throwing a javelin a long way or lifting heavy weights. Slow-twitch fibres are best for endurance activities such as long-distance running.

Changing the ratio

Some studies have suggested that, with appropriate training, it might be possible to increase the proportion of fast-twitch muscle fibres within a muscle, and thus increase the speed or strength of the muscle. However, research is still being carried out, and this has not yet been fully proved.

HEALTH FOCUS: Athletes and drugs

Most people have heard about athletes being tested for drugs that enhance their performance. These include **anabolic steroids**, such as nandrolone, which increase the size and strength of muscles. However, these can have serious long-term side effects, including liver damage and high blood pressure. For men, they can also include infertility and increased risk of prostate cancer; for women, disruption of the menstrual cycle. In adolescents, their use can stunt growth. Their use is banned in most competitive sports, and there are severe penalties for competitors found to have taken them.

 Here, a scientist working in the laboratories of the Italian National Olympic Committee in Rome, Italy is preparing a sportsperson's urine sample to be tested for the presence of anabolic steroids.

Body-building

Many people are not satisfied with the way their bodies look and want to change them in some way. Some want to have very strong, muscular bodies, and undertake special diets and training programmes to try to achieve their goal. In many cases, this does not cause a problem, but the use of drugs and some supplements can be dangerous. Training with heavy weights when young is also potentially harmful.

Body-building is the name given to the process of increasing muscle mass and strength. To achieve this muscle development, intensive training programmes of weightlifting are carried out, designed to concentrate on specific muscles and groups of muscles. Additionally, **protein**-rich diets provide the nutritional building blocks for muscle development. Together, weight training and diet can help to build up muscle strength and size.

 This body-builder is posing to demonstrate the strength and development of his muscles.

Teenage years

Many teenagers wish that they could be stronger and more athletic. They often also want to look more attractive. Although it may be tempting to try to improve your body, it is not a good idea to try it until you are older. Lifting heavy weights before your muscles are fully developed can cause muscle injuries. Weightlifting also puts pressure on the bones and joints and, although this helps to build bone in adults, it can inhibit bone growth in developing teenagers.

HEALTH FOCUS: Superman!

Some body-builders are very proud of their achievements, and enter competitions where they stand in different positions to display the size of specific muscle groups. One of the most famous body-builders was Charles Atlas, an Italian who immigrated to the USA. He developed a method of increasing muscle mass, called "Dynamic Tension", and used it to transform his weak body into a stronger, more masculine one. He won competitions, and became a model for famous artists and sculptors. By selling his method to other people, he became very rich and successful.

The best way to ensure that your body grows healthy and strong is to take part in lots of sporting activities. These will help to improve your dexterity and coordination, and to increase your speed and strength. A balanced diet and plenty of rest are also important. All these factors will help your body to develop healthily and naturally without being put under any unnecessary pressure and strain.

Drugs

Anabolic steroids are **synthetic** substances that are related to male **hormones**, and are used by some people to help build up muscle mass and strength. There are some medical conditions where these drugs can help, and they may be prescribed by a doctor. They can be taken orally, or injected, and are usually taken over cycles of weeks or months. Although they may have the desired effect on muscles, they can cause major side effects, including liver disease, kidney disease, high blood pressure, and psychological disorders, such as mood swings and depression. Problems suffered by men who take anabolic steroids include over-aggression, infertility, and baldness. Women who take anabolic steroids may become more masculine, growing facial hair, having a deeper voice, and becoming infertile due to disruption of the menstrual cycle. If teenagers take these drugs, it can prematurely stop their growth.

In this computer model of a molecule of the anabolic steroid drug nandrolone, the atoms are colour-coded: carbon (green), oxygen (red), and hydrogen (gold).

25

Muscle problems

Cramps

Most people have experienced the sudden, sharp pain of cramp. This happens when a single muscle in a group of muscles suddenly goes into spasm. The contraction may be over in a few seconds or may last for several minutes. It happens most frequently in the leg or foot, often while exercising or when lying in bed. Cramp may occur for a variety of different reasons; several factors seem to increase the risk, including low levels of fitness, dehydration, lack of certain **minerals**, poor blood circulation in the legs, and wearing high-heeled shoes.

The pain can usually be eased by stretching and gently massaging the affected muscle, because this can stimulate blood circulation. Eating a balanced diet containing plenty of fruit and vegetables reduces the likelihood of **vitamin** and mineral deficiency, and drinking plenty of water prevents dehydration. Wearing comfortable shoes with good arch support can also help to prevent cramp occurring. In some cases, a doctor may prescribe a substance called quinine to reduce the risk of cramp.

This athlete is suffering from cramp in his thigh muscle. Gentle massage can help to relieve the problem.

Tics

A tic is a repetitive, rapid, and involuntary contraction of a muscle. It usually involves muscles of the face and head, and leads to exaggeration of normal movements, such as blinking or nodding.

Tics usually begin in children between nine and twelve years of age, and they are more common in boys than in girls. Most tics last less than one year, some last longer and others may last for a lifetime. The reasons for a tic developing are not clear, but they are often associated with stress and anxiety, and get worse with strong emotions, such as anger.

In most cases, the tic will simply disappear without treatment. In some severe cases, such as Tourette's Syndrome (where a child may have many tics and a lack of coordination), medication can help to control the tic.

Sprains and strains

These two types of injury are often confused because they produce similar symptoms. A sprain is an injury to the strong cords (**ligaments**) that bind a joint together. A strain is an injury to a muscle or **tendon**. Both can be caused by sudden movements, awkward falls, or unaccustomed exercise. They cause local pain, swelling, and restricted movement of the injured area.

Sprains and strains are usually treated by rest, using ice packs to reduce swelling and a bandage for support until the injury has healed. Painkillers can be taken to take away any immediate pain.

Ageing and muscles

From around the age of 30, the amount of skeletal muscle in the body gradually reduces. Fibrous tissue and fatty tissue replace it. Muscle strength and the speed of reflexes also decrease with age. These changes take place partly because people tend to become less active as they get older. They can be stopped and even reversed if older people undertake endurance and strength training.

IN FOCUS: RIGOR MORTIS

Most people are aware that, after death, the body becomes stiff with rigor mortis. This happens because **myosin** filaments bind to **actin** filaments. They cannot detach themselves again, and so the muscles cannot contract or relax. It begins within a few hours of death and can last up to 24 hours. The stiffness disappears as the **protein** molecules in the muscles break down.

Muscles of the head, face and neck

Muscles of the head and neck hold the head in position and allow us to move it. The human face can show many different expressions, such as smiling and frowning. These are possible because we have a network of more than 30 muscles that work together to move different parts of our faces. These muscles are also important in chewing food and producing the sounds of speech.

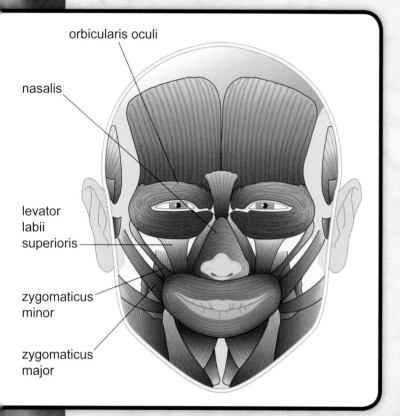

orbicularis oculi

nasalis

levator labii superioris

zygomaticus minor

zygomaticus major

The head is balanced on top of the spine. Pairs of muscles contract to allow us to nod our heads up and down, and other pairs contract to allow us to rotate it from side to side. It is held in its usual upright position by strong muscles in the neck.

Facial expressions

The muscles that control facial expressions are not just in the face, but also in the scalp and neck. They are attached to skin, bones, and **tendons**.

Around the eyes, nose, and mouth, rings of circular muscle called sphincters control the openings.

 This diagram shows the main muscles used when smiling.

IN FOCUS: THE TONGUE

The muscles of the tongue allow us to fold, curve, and squeeze the tongue, and to poke it out and in, up and down. These tongue muscles are essential for eating and for normal speech, but they can cause problems when a person is unconscious. The tongue can move backwards and block the airway, preventing normal breathing. This is often referred to as "swallowing one's tongue". When administering first aid to an unconscious person, it is important to check that this has not happened. When a **general anaesthetic** is administered to a patient in hospital, a narrow tube is inserted into the mouth to keep the airway open.

When we smile, the corners of the upper lip are lifted as muscles in the angles of the mouth contract. When we frown, other muscles pull down the corners of the mouth, wrinkle the forehead, and lower the eyelids. Smiling uses only seventeen muscles, whereas frowning uses 43!

Muscles in the sides of the cheeks move food around inside the mouth as we chew. These muscles are also important when we blow or suck – some jazz trumpeters overuse these cheek muscles so much that they lose their elasticity and automatically balloon outwards whenever the trumpeter begins to play.

Other muscles raise and lower the bottom jaw so that we can chew and speak.

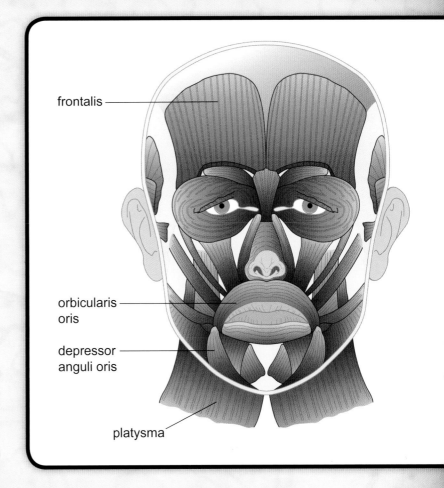

Problems

Some other problems can occur with the muscles of the face and head, including:

This diagram shows a sad face, indicating the main muscles used.

- **Headache**: tension headaches are most often caused by stress and tiredness. Painful contractions of muscles at the back of the neck and head cause discomfort, and pain spreads from the back of the head towards the eyes. The headache can get worse as blood vessels in the scalp constrict, reducing the blood supply and allowing waste products to build up. Tension headaches can often be eased by sleep or by taking painkillers.
- **Bell's palsy**: this is a one-sided paralysis of the face, due to damage to a facial nerve. Its cause is unknown but, in some cases, it may be triggered by extreme cold. Because of nerve damage, signals from the brain cannot reach the facial muscles. This means that the whole of one side of the face droops, so that the sufferer cannot wrinkle their forehead, close their eye, or pucker their lips, and they may have difficulty swallowing. The problem can be permanent, but most people recover fully in a few weeks.

Chest muscles

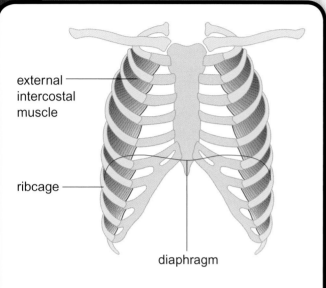

external intercostal muscle

ribcage

diaphragm

Breathing In
External intercostal muscles and diaphragm contract to increase space inside ribcage.

internal intercostal muscle

ribcage

diaphragm

Breathing Out
Internal intercostal muscles contract and diaphragm relaxes to decrease the space inside the ribcage.

The structure and shape of the chest is formed by the thoracic bones of the spine, the ribs, and the sternum (breastbone). The muscles attached to these bones allow us to breathe. Some also help upper body movements, and some with abdominal functions.

Breathing

- External intercostal muscles are attached to the bottom of one rib and to the top of the rib below. When they contract, all the ribs are lifted upwards and outwards.
- Internal intercostal muscles are also attached to the bottom of one rib and to the top of the rib below, but they run at a different angle to the external intercostal muscles. When these contract, all the ribs are forced downwards and inwards.
- The diaphragm is a large, dome-shaped sheet of tendon surrounded by a ring of muscle; it forms a partition between the chest and the abdomen. When the diaphragm contracts, it flattens and moves downwards. When it relaxes, it moves upwards and regains its dome shape.

Breathing in and out

- Breathing in: together, the contraction of the diaphragm and external intercostal muscles increase the space inside the ribcage, and air is sucked into the lungs.
- Breathing out: when the diaphragm relaxes and the internal intercostal muscles contract, the space inside the ribcage decreases, and air is forced out of the lungs.

 These diagrams show how the chest muscles help us to breathe in and out.

IN FOCUS: DIAPHRAGM

The diaphragm also has other important functions. When it contracts and moves downwards, it pushes on the organs of the abdomen and increases the pressure inside the abdomen. This can help to push waste out of the rectum and urine out of the bladder. The diaphragm can also help in childbirth, by forcing the baby out of the mother's body. When we lift heavy weights, we rely on the extra downward pressure that the diaphragm can exert.

Opera singers are trained to use their diaphragms to help them to exert very precise control over their breathing.

Problems

Some problems can occur with the chest muscles, including:

- **Stitch**: when you are running, the diaphragm may become short of oxygen and waste products may build up. You feel a sharp pain in your side, called a "stitch", as the diaphragm becomes fatigued. After a short rest, the pain goes and you can carry on running.
- **Hiccup**: most people have suffered from hiccups at some time. They happen when the regular, rhythmic contractions of the diaphragm are disturbed. Short, irregular, and uncontrollable contractions of the diaphragm cause the short, sharp intakes of breath that we call hiccups.
- **Paralysis**: this occurs when damage to nerves prevents signals from the brain reaching muscles, so the muscles do not contract and relax. Paralysis of the chest muscles makes breathing impossible. This can occur as the result of an accident or an infection, for example, polio. A heart-lung machine can take over and "breathe" artificially to keep the patient alive.
- **Anaesthetic**: when a patient is given a **general anaesthetic**, they are usually given a muscle relaxant drug as well. This relaxes all the muscles and makes surgery easier. It also makes it impossible to breathe, because the chest muscles cannot contract. The anaesthetist controls the patient's oxygen levels using a ventilator. When the operation is over, another drug is given to reverse the effects of the muscle relaxant, and the patient is able to breathe normally again.

Heart muscles

The heart is made from **cardiac muscle**. This specialized **involuntary muscle** contracts regularly and continually throughout our lives, ensuring that blood circulates to every part of our bodies. The heart beats roughly 70 times every minute, 100,000 times every day, 35 million times a year … if you live to be 70 years old, your heart will have beaten 2.5 billion times!

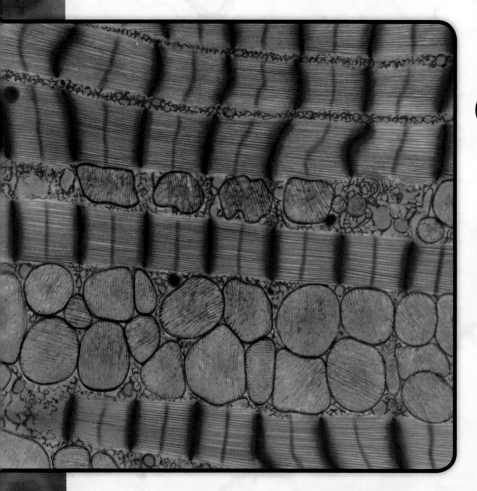

This photo-micrograph shows the internal structure of cardiac muscle. The tissue is **striated**, like skeletal muscle, but the fibres are interlinked, rather than parallel.

Cardiac muscle

Cardiac muscle is found only in the heart. It is made up from the same **myofibril** and **protein** components as skeletal muscle, but the muscle **fibres** are organized in a different way. In skeletal muscle, the muscle fibres all run parallel to each other, and do not cross or join. In cardiac muscle, the fibres are branched and interlinked, forming a dense network of muscle tissue.

The contraction of cardiac muscle is partly regulated by nervous signals, but cardiac muscle is also able to contract rhythmically without these signals. Within the heart wall, the muscle fibres are coordinated to contract, so that the movements of the heart chambers are synchronized and blood is pumped efficiently.

Heart attack

Cardiac muscle needs a plentiful supply of oxygen to maintain its contractions. Coronary arteries bring blood to the heart muscle, supplying it with **nutrients** and oxygen, and removing waste products. If the coronary arteries become blocked and the blood supply is interrupted, the contractions of the heart muscle become irregular and may stop altogether. This is a heart attack.

The patterns of contraction of muscle fibres can become irregular and lose their coordination. This causes feeble twitching, called fibrillation, instead of strong contractions. The heart chambers cannot contract properly, so blood is not pumped efficiently, which may result in death. Rhythm disturbances can often be treated with drugs. Equipment called a defibrillator can be used to administer an electric shock, stimulating the muscle fibres to regain their coordination.

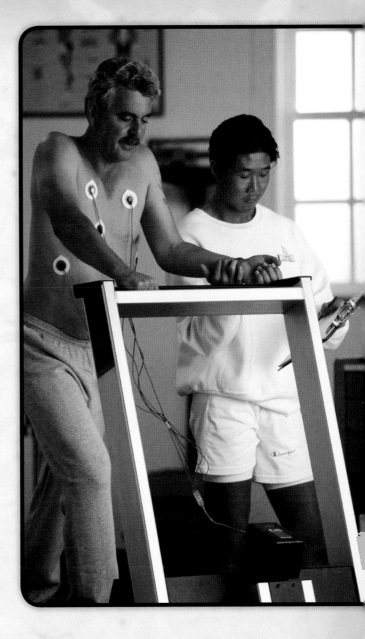

This patient's heartbeat is being monitored as he exercises. This helps doctors to assess how efficiently his heart is working. →

HEALTH FOCUS: Look after your heart

Like all muscle, the more you use the heart, the stronger it becomes. Regular **aerobic** exercise can help to keep the heart in excellent condition and reduce the risk of heart disease in later life.

Alcohol and smoking can both lead to heart problems, so it makes sense to avoid them. Being very overweight puts an extra strain on the heart; being underweight can lead to the breakdown of the heart muscle. A well-balanced diet and exercise both play an important part in maintaining a healthy body weight.

Abdominal muscles

The wall of the abdomen contains many muscles, which are arranged in layers. They control movements of the skeleton, maintaining posture and balance. They are also involved with assisting the functions of some internal organs.

Abdominal wall

The abdominal wall supports and protects the internal organs of the abdomen. A strong **tendon**, the linea alba, runs vertically down the midline of the body, from the sternum to the front of the pelvis (pubic bone). Four layers of muscle are built up around this tendon, acting as a corset around the abdomen. The outermost layer is the external abdominal oblique muscle. Fibres run forwards and downwards from the ribs, and are attached to the linea alba in the centre. The next layer is the internal abdominal oblique muscle. **Fibres** run forwards and upwards from each side of the pelvis to the linea alba. Below these muscles is the transverse abdominis muscle, running horizontally from the spine to the linea alba. The innermost layer of the abdominal wall is the rectus abdominis muscle, running vertically from the ribs to the pubic bone.

The contraction of muscles of the abdominal wall increases the pressure within the abdomen and on the abdominal organs. This is important in urination, **defecation**, and in childbirth.

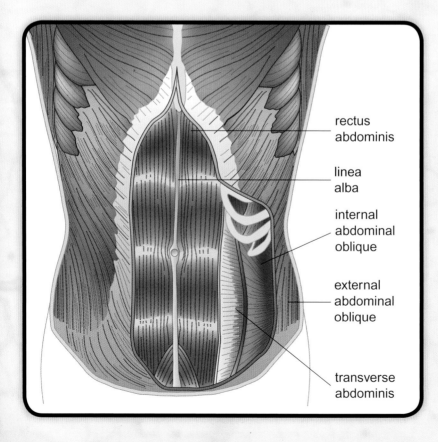

rectus abdominis

linea alba

internal abdominal oblique

external abdominal oblique

transverse abdominis

The abdominal wall is made up of four strong muscle layers and the linea alba tendon.

HEALTH FOCUS: Hernia

A hernia arises when an area of the abdominal wall is weak. Part of the small intestine may protrude through some or all of the layers of the wall, causing a lump. Hernias usually occur near the groin (inguinal hernias) or near the navel (umbilical hernias). Hernias are more common in men than in women. Some people are born with a weakness that makes it likely they will develop a hernia. In other cases, hernias can be caused by a serious, persistent cough that causes high pressure within the abdomen, or by heavy lifting. Hernias can be repaired surgically, often under **local anaesthetic** using a technique called "keyhole surgery".

Pelvic muscles

There are two main groups of pelvic muscles, making up the pelvic diaphragm and the perineum. Together, these form the floor of the pelvis, supporting the pelvic organs. They help to maintain the internal abdominal pressure, and control defecation and urination. They are also important in childbirth.

Lower back muscles

On each side, at the back of the body, a strong muscle (the quadratus lumborum) is attached to the pelvis, the **lumbar vertebrae**, and the twelfth rib. Contracting one muscle results in flexion on that side of the body. Together, these muscles help to provide stability.

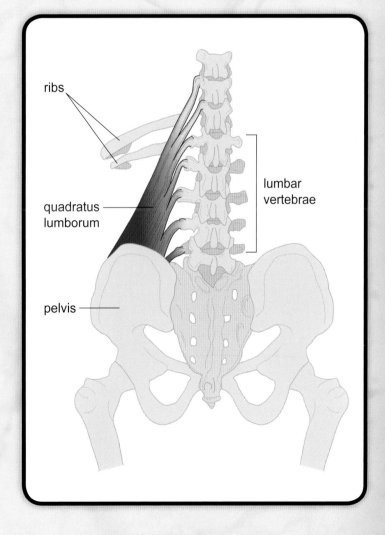

ribs

quadratus lumborum

lumbar vertebrae

pelvis

The quadratus lumborum muscle allows side to side movements and provides stability.

Internal involuntary muscles

Some internal organs and vessels contain **involuntary muscles**. These are **smooth muscles**, involved in internal processes that are essential to the normal functioning of the body.

The alimentary canal

- oesophagus
- liver
- stomach
- pancreas
- duodenum
- colon

The walls of the alimentary canal contain smooth muscles that contract to push the food along.

Digestive system

The alimentary canal is a long tube that makes up most of the digestive system. Although there are variations in size and surface detail, the basic structure is the same throughout its length:

- The outer layer (adventitia or serosa) is a thin layer of connective tissue.
- Beneath this is a layer of longitudinal muscle **fibres**, which run along the length of the wall.
- Next comes a layer of circular muscle fibres, which run in rings around the wall.
- Below this is a thick layer of connective tissue (submucosa), which contains nerves and blood vessels.
- The innermost layer (mucosa) produces **mucus** that keeps food slippery, helping it to slide easily along.
- At the centre is the lumen, the space through which food moves. The muscle fibres in the wall of the alimentary canal contract regularly, creating a rippling wave-like movement called peristalsis. This movement pushes food along the canal.

Blood vessels

Blood vessels carry the blood from the heart, around the body and back to the heart again. The heart pumps blood out at great pressure and so the vessels that carry blood away from the heart have to be very strong to withstand the force. The arteries have very strong walls, made up of three layers:

- a thick outer layer of collagen fibres
- a thick middle layer of elastic and muscle fibres, arranged in rings
- a thin lining layer.

The walls of major arteries are elastic, allowing them to stretch as the heart pumps blood into them, and contract when the heart relaxes.

Veins carry blood back to the heart. They have thinner walls than arteries, because they carry blood at a lower pressure. Their walls also have three layers:
- a thin outer layer of collagen fibres
- a thin middle layer, containing few muscle fibres
- a thin lining layer.

Airways
The bronchioles are narrow passages within the lungs. Their walls contain rings of smooth muscle, forming spiral bands. The bronchioles do not contain any supporting material so, if the muscles contract, the airways can narrow and close. This happens in an asthma attack. An **allergic reaction** can cause histamine release, and this makes these muscles contract, causing breathing difficulties. Bronchodilator drugs can be taken, usually via an inhaler, to prevent spasm of the bronchiole muscles.

HEALTH FOCUS: Goosebumps
Smooth muscles, each called an arrector pili, are attached to the dermis of the skin and to the side of each hair follicle. When these muscles are relaxed, the hairs leave the skin at a fairly shallow angle and lay flat. When the muscles contract, the hairs are pulled up straight and stand upright. This often happens when we are cold or scared, and we usually refer to the effect as "goosebumps". Rubbing the skin vigorously usually makes the goosebumps disappear.

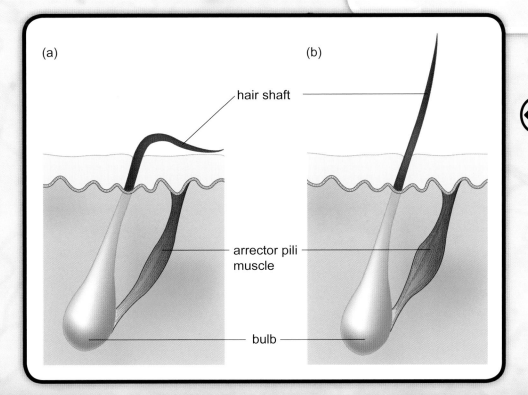

(a) (b)

hair shaft

arrector pili muscle

bulb

In the picture on the left (a), the muscle is relaxed and the hair is lying flat. In the picture on the right (b), the muscle has contracted and pulled the hair upright.

Arm and hand muscles

The muscles that move the bones of the arm and hand allow a wide range of movements. We can hurl a ball with great strength using the full power of the shoulder, and we can make tiny, precise movements with each finger.

Moving the upper arm

Several groups of muscles control movement of the shoulder joint. The four rotator cuff tendons are attached to the shoulder blade (scapula) and the upper arm bone (humerus), preventing dislocation and instability. The deltoid muscles form the rounded shape of the shoulder and are attached to the scapula, humerus, and collarbone (clavicle). The pectoral muscles of the chest are attached to the clavicle, sternum, ribs, and humerus. Together, these muscles move the shoulder joint in three directions – up and down, side to side, and backwards and forwards, allowing complete rotation and circular movements. The muscles are powerful, which allows the upper arm to exert great force.

Moving the lower arm

The arm is hinged at the elbow, allowing the lower arm to be flexed (raised) or extended (lowered). Two muscles control this movement – the biceps contracts to raise the lower arm and the triceps contracts to lower the arm. This movement is described in greater detail on page 18.

 This diagram shows some of the major muscles that move the shoulder and upper arm.

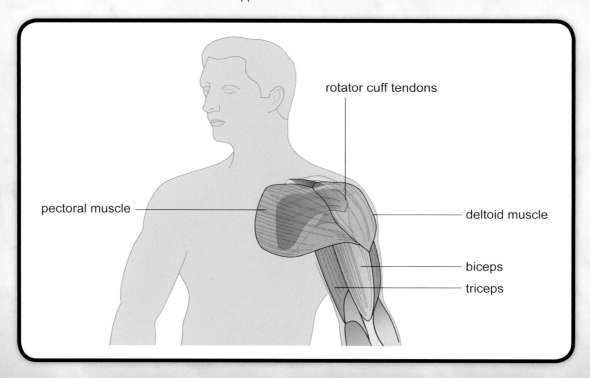

rotator cuff tendons

pectoral muscle

deltoid muscle

biceps

triceps

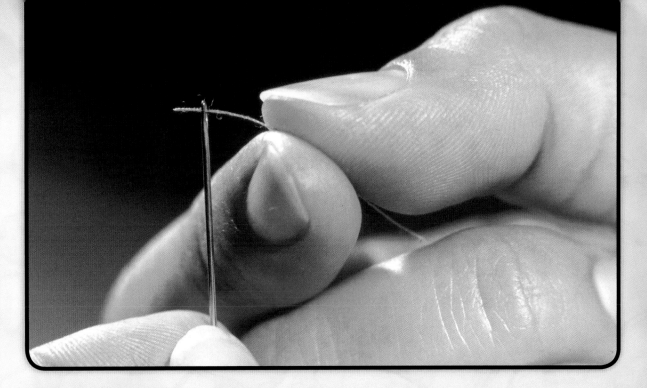

↑ The human hand is capable of carrying out very tiny, precise movements.

Moving the wrist

The complex wrist joints allow us to lift our hand up and down, and to move it from side to side. We can also rotate it so that the palm faces up or down. Many different muscles are involved in moving the wrist. They are attached to the humerus and lower arm bones, and to the carpal bones of the wrist.

Moving the hand

The fingers are hinged and we can move them up and down, as well as bending them at each individual joint. Each finger and thumb is controlled by the contraction of its own individual muscles. Muscles of the palm and back of the hand allow us to spread the fingers apart.

The human thumb is capable of a special movement called opposition, meaning that the thumb can be brought across the palm of the hand to touch the little finger. This movement is only found in humans and some other primates, and it allows us to grasp objects with great precision.

HEALTH FOCUS:
Carpal tunnel syndrome

The carpal tunnel is a narrow channel in the wrist through which nerves and **tendons** pass. Sometimes, these nerves and tendons can get squashed, causing pain and weakness in the hand. This is called carpal tunnel syndrome. It can be due to injury or infection, but is more often due to excessive repetitive exercises, such as playing the piano, or using a computer keyboard or typewriter. Usually, the symptoms can be cured simply by rest and by avoiding the exercise that caused the problem, but occasionally surgery may be necessary.

Leg and foot muscles

The muscles that control the movement of the hip joint are the largest and most powerful in the body. They provide stability for the joint, and power to move the whole body. The muscles of the legs and feet also allow us to stand upright, by helping to maintain our posture and, by operating in sequence, they allow us to walk and run.

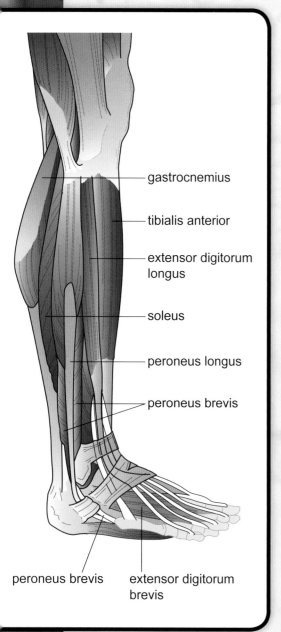

gastrocnemius

tibialis anterior

extensor digitorum longus

soleus

peroneus longus

peroneus brevis

peroneus brevis

extensor digitorum brevis

Moving the thigh

The hip joint is a strong ball and socket joint, allowing the thigh a wide range of movements. Strong muscles surround the joint to provide stability and prevent dislocation. The gluteus maximus muscle is used when powerful movements are needed, such as when climbing stairs, running, and jumping.

Moving the lower leg

When the hamstring muscles at the back of the thigh contract, the lower leg is pulled back, and when muscles at the front of the thigh contract, the lower leg is pulled forward.

Moving the foot

When muscles at the back of the lower leg contract, the heel is raised, and when muscles at the front of the lower leg contract, the ball of the foot and toes are raised. Several muscles work together to allow the foot to rotate freely at the ankle joint. Within the foot, strong muscles contract to maintain the arch of the foot, and to allow it to flex as we walk. Individual muscles move each toe in a similar manner to the muscles in the hand that move the fingers. However, unlike the toes of some other primates, the big toe operates exactly as the other toes and cannot move in opposition like the thumb.

 This diagram shows some of the major muscles that move the leg and foot.

Common injuries

Because we use the muscles of the legs and feet so much, they are often injured, especially in sporting activities. Some common injuries include:

- **Groin strain**: this is most common in activities that involve quick sprints, such as soccer, tennis, and running. Muscles deep in the groin may be stretched or torn, causing pain. With rest and **physiotherapy**, the injury usually heals completely.
- **Pulled hamstring**: the hamstring is one of the strong muscles at the back of the thigh. It may be strained or partially torn by running very hard, or by an abrupt start or stop. There is usually bruising and intense pain. The risk of hamstring injury can be reduced by proper training and adequate stretching exercises before and after any activity.
- **Shinsplints**: tendinitis causes pain along the length of the shin bones. This is usually the result of running on hard surfaces in poor shoes, or after a sudden burst of intense exercise after a long period of inactivity.
- **Plantar fasciitis**: also called "painful heel syndrome", this is the most common cause of heel pain in runners. It is usually due to the repeated impact of the foot on the ground, causing inflammation of the plantar aponeurosis (flat sheet of tendon) where it attaches to the heel

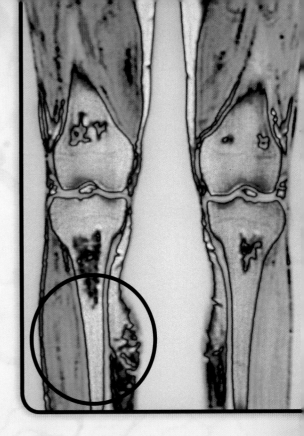

This coloured magnetic resonance imaging (MRI) scan shows a torn calf muscle (the bulge on the right side of the leg at lower left). Treatment is by resting the muscle, applying ice and compression, and keeping the leg raised.

HEALTH FOCUS: Achilles injury

The Achilles **tendon** can be injured in several ways, and the injury can be at the point where the tendon is attached to the heel bone or just above the heel bone. Strains, minor tears, and inflammations cause pain that may develop slowly or appear suddenly; the pain is usually worst when the tendon is stretched, such as when running uphill. Sometimes the Achilles tendon may snap, but it can be sewn back together or repaired using a graft taken from elsewhere in the body.

Minor injuries can be caused by poor sports shoes, so it is important to check that your shoes fit well and that there is no friction between the shoes and the back of your ankle. Treatment depends on the extent of the injury. X-rays may be needed to check that there is no damage to the heel bone. For minor injuries, an injection may be given to reduce inflammation. Rest, heat treatment, and ultrasound all help to accelerate healing.

Muscle diseases and problems

Motor neurone disease

Motor neurone disease is not a disease of the muscles themselves, but it has the effect of preventing muscle contraction. Muscles can only contract in response to a signal from the brain. These signals are carried along nerves called motor neurones. In motor neurone disease, the neurones slowly break down and waste away. At first, it may cause only minor difficulties, such as weakness and stiffness. Slowly, it affects more muscles and difficulties become greater, affecting functions such as speech and swallowing. The cause of motor neurone disease is unknown and there is no effective long-term treatment. In some people, it is fatal in a short period of time, while others, such as the physicist Professor Stephen Hawking, can live for many years.

Myasthenia gravis

Myasthenia gravis is much more common in women than in men, and causes extreme fatigue. It is an autoimmune disease, which means that the immune system recognizes parts of the body as foreign and attacks them. The immune system produces chemicals, called antibodies, against the **acetylcholine** receptors of the muscle **fibres**. These antibodies bind to the receptors and block them. When acetylcholine is released, the receptors do not detect it and, therefore, the muscles do not contract. Some drug treatments can be given to increase the levels of acetylcholine in the body, and steroids can be given to prevent antibody production.

IN FOCUS: TECHNOLOGICAL SOLUTIONS

Scientists are working on many different ideas to try to make life easier for people who are paralysed. One promising line of research involves implanting a tiny electrode in the patient's brain. This picks up signals within the brain and sends them to a computer. If the person thinks about carrying out an action, such as moving a computer mouse, the electrode detects the signal and sends the instruction to the computer and the action is carried out. Using this technology, patients have been able to perform simple actions such as using a computer, changing television channels, and even controlling robotic arms and hands.

Muscular dystrophy

Muscular dystrophy is the name given to a group of inherited diseases, all of which cause muscle weakness. The most common, and most severe, is Duchenne's muscular dystrophy, which affects boys almost exclusively. Initially, the muscles of the thigh and pelvis are weak, making it difficult to stand and to walk. Later, other muscles become weak, affecting other movements. If the muscles involved in breathing or the heart muscle are affected, the patient may die. Treatment by exercise and **physiotherapy** can help, but most sufferers die at an early age.

Paralysis

Again, this is not a disease of the muscles, but is caused by the failure of signals from the brain to reach the muscles. Spinal injuries can cause paralysis, because damage to the spinal cord disrupts signals to and from the brain. If the injury is in the neck, all four limbs may be paralysed and the patient is said to be tetraplegic (tetra is the Greek word for four) or quadraplegic. A lower spinal injury may mean that the person can still move their arms, but their legs and lower body are paralysed; they are said to be paraplegic. A stroke (a blood clot in the brain) can cause paralysis. Usually, this affects just one side of the body, and is often only temporary.

Spinal cord injuries can result in paralysis. Christopher Reeve, who starred as the film hero "Superman", suffered a serious spinal cord injury when he fell from his horse. Stem cell therapies that may promote nerve regeneration are now offering new hope to patients paralysed by spinal cord injuries.

What can go wrong with my muscles?

This book has explained the different parts of the muscular system, why they are important and how they can be damaged by injury and illness. This page summarizes some of the problems that can affect the muscles. It also gives information about how each problem can be treated.

Illness or injury	Cause	Symptoms	Prevention	Treatment
tendinitis	inflammation of a tendon or its surrounding membrane	painful joint; may be swollen, with restriction of movement	avoid repetition of painful movement	rest; ice pack; anti-inflammatory drugs may be prescribed
extreme tension	damage to a tendon by overstretching or jerking	painful joint; may be swollen, with restriction of movement	maintain a healthy lifestyle; avoid overstretching or jerking	rest; ice pack; support bandage; painkillers may be prescribed
cramp	sudden muscle spasm within a group of muscles	sudden pain that may last for a few seconds or longer	regular exercise; eat a healthy diet; drink plenty of water	gentle stretching and massage of affected muscles
sprain	injury to ligament due to an awkward fall or unaccustomed exercise	swollen painful joint, with restriction of movement	maintain a healthy lifestyle; avoid sudden excessive movements	rest; ice pack; support bandage; painkillers may be prescribed
strain	injury to muscle or tendon, often due to an awkward fall or to unaccustomed exercise	swollen painful joint, with restriction of movement	maintain a healthy lifestyle; avoid sudden excessive movements	rest; ice pack; support bandage; painkillers may be prescribed

Many problems can be avoided or prevented by maintaining a healthy lifestyle. Taking regular exercise and getting plenty of rest are important, as is eating a balanced diet. This is especially important in your teenage years, when your body is still developing. The table on page 44 tells you about some of the ways you can prevent muscle injury and illness.

Remember, if you think something is wrong with your body, you should always talk to a trained medical professional such as a doctor or a school nurse. Regular medical check-ups are an important part of maintaining a healthy body.

Find out more

Books to read

Move Your Body! (Body Talk), Steve Parker (Raintree, 2006)

Muscles and Skeletons (Our Bodies), Steve Parker (Wayland, 2004)

The Skeleton and Muscles (Exploring the Human Body), Carol Ballard (Franklin Watts, 2007)

Sports Science (Why Science Matters), Andrew Solway (Heinemann Library, 2009)

Websites to visit

http://www.bbc.co.uk/science/humanbody/body/factfiles/muscle_anatomy
Website with information about the muscles, including interactive activities.

http://kidshealth.org/teen/your_body/body_basics/bones_muscles_joints
Website for teenagers with information about muscles, maintaining healthy and strong muscles, and muscle problems.

http://www.kidsexercise.co.uk/WeightTrainingForTeens
Website with advice and information about healthy ways of exercising and building muscle strength.

http://www.biology4kids.com/files/systems_muscular
Website with information about muscles and how they work.

Glossary

acetylcholine chemical released by a nerve carrying a signal from the brain to a muscle

actin main protein of thin myofilaments

aerobic chemical reaction that uses oxygen

allergic reaction reaction by the body to an antigen to which it is sensitive, such as the runny nose and sore eyes of hay fever sufferers when exposed to pollen

amino acid one of the basic units of a protein molecule

anabolic steroid synthetic drug that increases muscle mass and strength

anaerobic chemical reaction that does not use oxygen

capillary delicate blood vessel running between veins and arteries

carbon fibre strong threads of carbon that can be woven into a very strong material

cardiac muscle muscle tissue of the heart

defecation removal of solid waste from the body

epimysium outer covering of a muscle

fascicle bundle of muscle fibres

fatigue tiring of a muscle due to build-up of waste products

fibre single muscle cell

general anaesthetic drugs given to send a patient to sleep and prevent them feeling anything

hormones chemicals made in the body. They travel around the body in the blood, and affect organs and tissues in a variety of ways.

involuntary muscle muscle that contracts without conscious control

ligament strong, elastic cord that binds joints together

local anaesthetic drug that numbs a small part of the body

lumbar relating to the lower back

mineral one of a number of chemicals needed by the body in very small amounts, for example, calcium and iron

motor end plate junction between a motor neurone and a muscle fibre

motor neuron nerve that carries signals from the brain to muscle

motor unit motor neurone and all the muscle fibres it stimulates

mucus sticky, slimy fluid that acts as a lubricant

myofibril thin strand inside a muscle fibre

myofilament strand of protein inside a myofibril

myosin main protein of thick myofilaments

nutrients part of our food that the body can use

physiotherapy exercises and other treatments to help recovery after injury

protein complex chemical that is a component of many of the body's structures

pulses edible seeds, such as peas, beans, and lentils

sarcolemma outer membrane covering of a muscle fibre

smooth muscle involuntary muscle of some internal organs and vessels

striated striped

synthetic made artificially to be like a natural product

tendon strong, inelastic, fibrous cord that attaches muscle to bone

vertebrae segments of the backbone

vitamin one of a number of complex chemicals that the body needs in very small amounts

voluntary muscle muscle that is under conscious control

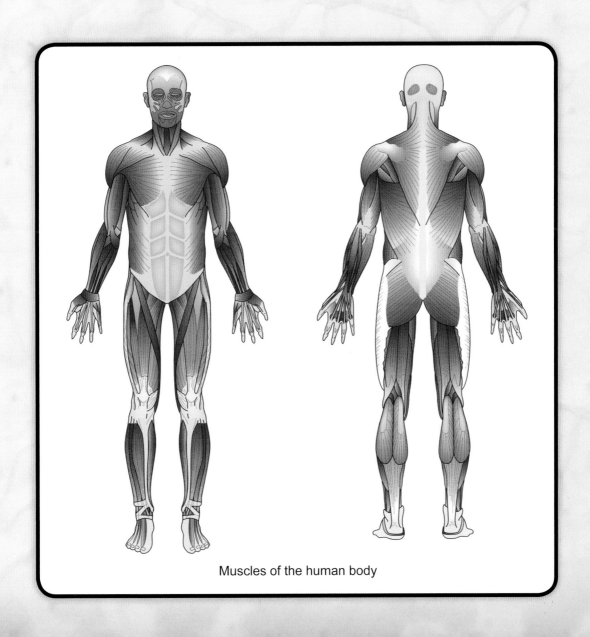

Muscles of the human body

Index